REVOLUTIONS

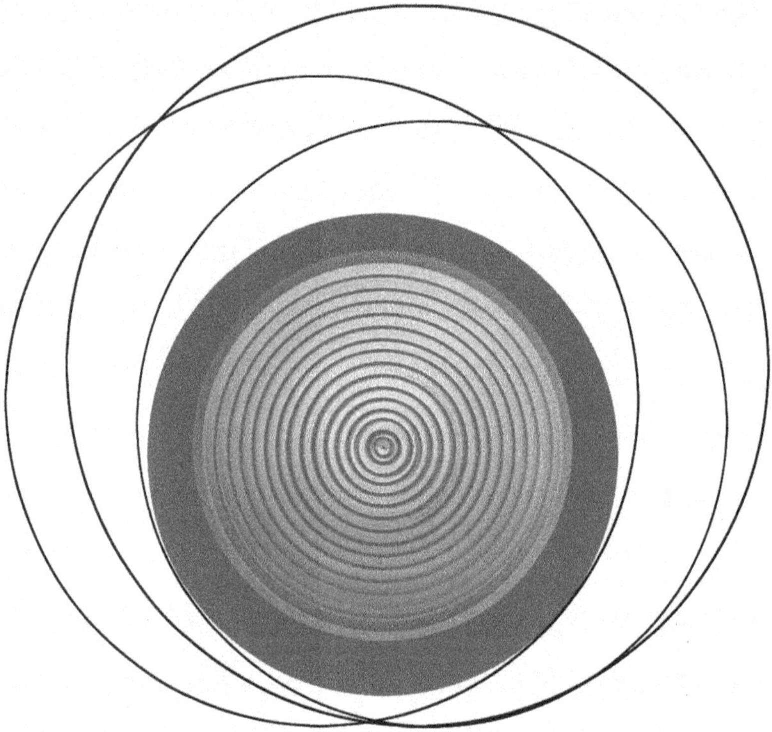

REVOLUTIONS

REVOLUTIONS

REVOLUTIONS

REVOLUTIONS

REVOLUTIONS

REVOLUTIONS

REVOLUTIONS

HAJER MIRWALI

Poems

Talonbooks

Talonbooks
9259 Shaughnessy Street, Vancouver, British Columbia, Canada V6P 6R4
talonbooks.com

Talonbooks is located on xʷməθkʷəy̓əm, Sḵwx̱wú7mesh, and səlilwətaɬ Lands.

First printing: 2025

Typeset in Arno and Odile
Printed and bound in Canada on 100% post-consumer recycled paper

Talonbooks acknowledges the financial support of the Canada Council for the Arts, the Government of Canada through the Canada Book Fund, and the Province of British Columbia through the British Columbia Arts Council and the Book Publishing Tax Credit.

Library and Archives Canada Cataloguing in Publication

Title: Revolutions : poems / Hajer Mirwali.
Names: Mirwali, Hajer, author.
Identifiers: Canadiana 20240435230 | ISBN 9781772016505 (softcover)
Subjects: LCGFT: Poetry.
Classification: LCC PS8626.I793 R48 2025 | DDC C811/.6—dc23

For Mama and xxxxxxx

For Baba, I chose the number seven for you

While waiting, I become obsessed with observing
the many possibilities ...

—MAHMOUD DARWISH

"While Waiting" (2007) (translated by Fady Joudah)

I wanted to be a good mother, the mother says.
Sometimes you weren't, the daughter says.

Sometimes you weren't a good daughter either, the mother says
and the daughter says, I wanted to be good

—HAYAN CHARARA

"Mother and Daughter" (2016)

Are you still on the highway You said the movie starts at seven Where did you go after I'm sure you went somewhere else It's almost twelve Where are you Baba's asleep so I'm going to say you came home then left again for the gym You know how he is No I can't just say that Hek a7san I don't want to hear anything If he asks say you went to the gym He's not going to pay attention to your clothes Yalla come home It's so late Ya binti why do you do this to me

3AIB

being a girl is white ash from the firepit on my black cardigan her black jeans our black hair except for xxxxxxx who has it dyed a light brown and xxxxxxx and xxxxxxx who wear hijabs we had to wash our bodies twice got past the chlorine and sunscreen to the layer of smoke finally it was time to eat we wondered should we put a cover over our bikinis would it be 3aib the 5aalas are right there what will they think (old Arabs always say what they think) finally our skin was showing whether it was 3aib or not 3aib to wear a tampon to buy a low-cut shirt to make eye contact to suck on a lollipop in the car when the windows aren't tinted anything above the knee is 3aib we squished four in the back seat 3aib sat on xxxxxxx's lap we listened to a song that hurts your ears but makes you feel like you're at the climax of a really good indie film xxxxxxx said I love dealing with teenage problems in my twenties xxxxxxx said I love to be fully inside

myself is 3aib

we rolled 3aib up smoked it got so fucking 3aib holy 3aib it was 3aib everything is 3aib say it with me now everything that makes you different from other girls is sitting with your legs open is not kissing all the 5aalas when you enter a room is shisha and dancing and slutty and embarrassing and laughing and armpit and guitar and transparency and desire and reproductive health and bras and red lipstick and not being sad enough and being sad 3aib cried in the car talking about her mom the rest of us cried hearing her crying is 3aib moving far away is 3aib getting married next summer is 3aib spending the whole night fixing the fire every twenty minutes the train goes by we wait for it to pass before we start again

CYCLE GENERATOR

xxxxxxx wants to push her finger [redacted] sand until she touches the box

box wants to xxxxxxx her push [redacted] finger until she sands the touch

touch wants to box her xxxxxxx [redacted] push until she fingers the sand

sand wants to touch her box [redacted] xxxxxxx until she pushes the finger

finger wants to sand her touch [redacted] box until she xxxxxxx's the push

push wants to finger her sand [redacted] touch until she boxes the xxxxxxx

xxxxxxx wants to push her finger [redacted] sand until she touches the box

Mona Hatoum

+ and –

1994

Wood, sand, stainless steel, and motor

8 × 30 × 30 cm (3 ¼ × 11 ¾ × 11 ¾ in.)

her hand at one
her hand at one
her hand at one
her hand at one
her hand at one
her hand at one
her hand at one
her hand at one
her hand at one
her hand at one
her hand at one
her hand at one
her hand at one

seven

at

hand

her

I sit in the sand with xxxxxxx

We wait together

Waiting is generational

Waiting breeds returns

MEETING + AND -

MEETING + AND -
MEETING + AND -
MEETING + AND -
MEETING + AND -
MEETING + AND -
MEETING + AND -

Notes from the *Open Works* exhibition at
La Pedrera, Barcelona

January 18

On the plane Mama asks if xxxxxxx has a boyfriend. We are two women talking about a girl we are worried for. We eat the halal meal. We scroll past a photo on Instagram think how ugly that girl's shoes are. We sleep on our shoulder. We feel our warmth doubling. We forget our obligation to split. We remember a few months ago that outdoor movie screening with limited parking the first time in our lives anger revealed to one another our naked body behind the curtain.

Perhaps it was the excitement of travel or being far away from everyone but once we passed security in Toronto I felt my arms conjugate with hers.

her hand at two
her hand at two
her hand at two

her hand at two
her hand at two
her hand at two
her hand at two
her hand at two
her hand at two
her hand at two
her hand at two
her hand at two
her hand at two
her hand at two
her hand at two
her hand at two
her hand at two
her hand at two
her hand at two
her hand at two
her hand at two
her hand at two
her hand at two
her hand at two
her hand at two
her hand at two
her hand at two
her hand at two
her hand at two
her hand at two
her hand at two
her hand at two
her hand at two
her hand at two
her hand at two
her hand at two
her hand at two
her hand at two
her hand at two

her hand at eight

her hand at two
her hand at two
her hand at two
her hand at two
her hand at two
her hand at two

her hand at two
her hand at two
her hand at two

her hand at two
her hand at two

her hand at two

January 19

Gaudí's warriors protected the rooftop of Casa Mila. Everything was soft. I looked at the sky through a circle. I followed the spiral stairs to become smaller and smaller. I held my mother's bag. Her hand fell under the square of sunlight as she passed it to me.

We visited the exhibition last. She walked to the end where + *and* – was while I slowly looked at the rest of the art. When she returned she was disappointed for me. Your piece is this small, she said, holding her thumb and index finger close together.

The blades create two borders. Linear border separating grooved sand from smooth sand. Circular border where sand has accumulated at blades' ends.

Does a circle mean you can return?
Does a circle mean you can't leave?

+ *and* – as argument:

I am emptying of ways to lie to Mama
opening more holes for my lies.

her
hand
at
nine

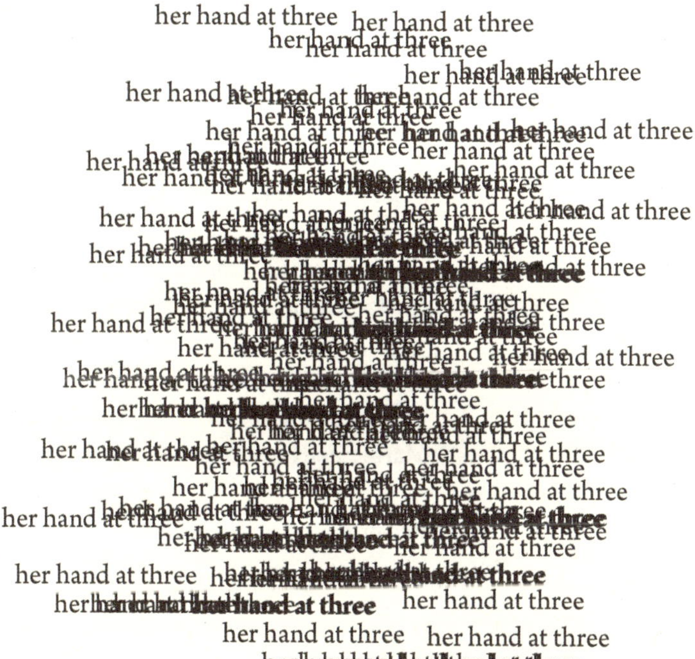

January 20

Because I am serrated, I am not. Dreaming
into the state of observing grooves
immortalized in the bed of sand.

At another museum, I find sand. Along the
streets of the Gothic Quarter, sand. Under a
porcelain bull, sand. Because I am smooth, I
am not.

With + *and* – today and without.

A marble figure of a man reclined moves
more inside me. I wait for Mama to wander
to the next room. I cry for his stillness.
Tendons on a marble foot not unlike my
tendons. I am never not.

Marble frustration   sand.
Marble dick imprint   sand.
Marble belly button   sand.

Because I am always and never away.

her hand at ten

her hand at four
her hand at four
her hand at four

her hand at four
her hand at four
her hand at four
her hand at four
her hand at four
her hand at four
her hand at four
her hand at four
her hand at four

her hand at four
her hand at four
her hand at four
her hand at four
her hand at four
her hand at four

her hand at four

her hand at four
her hand at four
her hand at four
her hand at four
her hand at four
her hand at four
her hand at four
her hand at four
her hand at four

January 21

A reality mobile continually transforming. Open works encompass, implore. Foreign to fluorescent light until even that is paled again.

Today throbs. Centre of the circling vibration swells inside a balloon dream of slivered light seizing ceaseless power.

\+ *and* – revolutions language
giving
giving
giving
with any arm it can procure.

I oscillate.

Concentric strokes compress around my head. It takes thirty seconds to complete one revolution.

Another visitor: This is so soothing.

When Mama calls I say I'm still at the gallery so I can order my ham croquette and Mahou. Pretend they give freedom.

I write for one revolution:

Revolution
Revolution
Revolution
Revolution
Revolution
Revolution
Revolution
Revolution
Revolution
Revolution
Revolution

Waiting
Waiting
Waiting
Waiting
Waiting
Waiting
Waiting
Waiting
Waiting
Waiting
Waiting
Waiting
Waiting
Waiting

Presence
Presence
Presence
Presence
Presence
Presence
Presence
Presence
Presence
Presence
Presence
Presence
Presence

Border
Border
Border
Border
Border
Border
Border
Border

Border
Border
Border
Border
Border
Border
Border
Border
Border

Absence
Absence
Absence
Absence
Absence
Absence
Absence
Absence
Absence
Absence
Absence
Absence
Absence
Absence

January 22

In 1994 Mama gave birth to me in Amman on her way from Baghdad to Richmond Hill and Mona with wood sand metal electric motor transported us to the first home we were exiled from. Two daughters of a revolutionary split. Two mothers of a contracting uterus waiting to be Palestinian again.

Past noon. Shadows cast by a swinging mobile are longer, higher.

Repetitive sounds mimic Mona's repletion: whirring projector light, needle hitting copper thread. Mama held my slippery body to her chest. Mama's slippery body on my chest. She asks if I have ever listened to + *and* –. Grains of sand flowing through one another. Every daughter grain resorbs her mother grain as first foreign body. Lives her whole life with that inside her.

I later fix "Mona's repletion" to repetition to repletion. Mona so near bursting every line she erases reconfigures its genes into another line.

Every time Mama asks what I am writing
I only say + *and* –.

her

hand

at

eleven

her hand at five

January 23

+ *and* –, I have come too far to feel nothing.

Wait for me in the dark room. Strip apart my arms. Hear me change. Daughter of + *and* –. Daughter. Daughter. More daughterly with every rotation.

What are you writing about?

A sculpture.

Yes?

Yes, a very good daughter who loves
her motherlands and her God.

A daughter more and less.

A daughter + and –.

Never the same twice.

Sand
Sand
Sand
Sand
Sand
Sand
Sand
Sand
Sand
Sand
Sand
Sand
Sand
Sand
Sand
Sand
Sand

Circular
Circular
Circular
Circular
Circular
Circular
Circular
Circular
Circular
Circular
Circular
Circular
Circular
Circular
Circular
Circular

xxxxxxx
xxxxxxx
xxxxxxx
xxxxxxx
xxxxxxx
xxxxxxx
xxxxxxx

CYCLE GENERATOR

revealed [redacted] another our naked body behind [redacted] curtain

curtain [redacted] revealed our another naked body [redacted] behind

behind [redacted] curtain our revealed another naked [redacted] body

body [redacted] behind our curtain revealed another [redacted] naked

naked [redacted] body our behind curtain revealed [redacted] another

another [redacted] naked our body behind curtain [redacted] revealed

revealed [redacted] another our naked body behind [redacted] curtain

HOURGLASS PROCEDURE

(twenty-minute poems to be read in two directions)

+ *and* – plus and minus plu sand minus pl us and min us

Make your body as light as possible so your footsteps become silent

The trick is to let the garage door fully close before you enter the house

After all the wars Baba's a very light sleeper

Last night I had to get to my room without waking him up

I don't know if I'm used to anything

My lover said, You're just not used to a liberal Arab dad

He'll be leaving tomorrow

Not worrying about how late I'm at his house

How long it takes to come

+ *and* – as the present moment

An hourglass that never empties or fills

I'll be sitting for an hour before I realize I've been tensing my legs the whole time

I don't know how to enjoy anything

Have I stopped caring about Palestine?

I want to go skating

Want to eat hand-pulled noodles

To live alone

I want to be a mother

Again I want to listen to the oud

Naseer Shamma would not have written “Layl Baghdad” if it weren’t for the mirage

If it weren't for the mirage

Then it was just us

I dreamed of an apocalypse, finding xxxxxxx alive under water

In my dream I was wearing three animal-print items: a bikini, cardigan, pyjama pants

My new Picasso line drawing and strands of hair on the shower wall look the same

+ and –

For one half of the hourglass to fill the other half must empty

OPEN GUIDE OF PALESTINE

OPEN GUIDE OF PALESTINE
OPEN GUIDE OF PALESTINE
OPEN GUIDE OF PALESTINE
OPEN GUIDE OF PALESTINE
OPEN GUIDE OF PALESTINE
OPEN GUIDE OF PALESTINE

In Jerusalem, and I mean within the ancient walls,
I walk from one epoch to another without a memory
to guide me.

—MAHMOUD DARWISH
"In Jerusalem" (2007) (translated by Fady Joudah)

Before having been I remember
returning to Al-8uds. Returning
in the present tense. I would love
returning. I am been returning.

Sand is falling through the mouth
in the fullest sense of the word:
already having fallen, waiting to fall
again. If business is getting better

we can be return for the first time.
In past tense once we are there. Sand
falling upwards like the Prophet's
footsteps to heaven: we will returning

to 8uds. Inshallah we did returns.
Where a mother distanced closer to God
is trying returned her wedding dress with
the rest of her future memories. Reaching

checkpoints. Unlike sand the full-body
turnstile is locked for single-direction use.
Sometimes locks completely protecting
against all past present future attacks.

The mother her dress the father his lungs
filling with water all trapped on one
side of the throat long enough for the
hospital to get farther and farther away.

The mother's pregnant granddaughter's
ten cm dilation told to wait her turn
while the Soldier of Death! finds the
perfect space between two bars

of the steel barricade to stick his rifle
through. The baby is being born some
year between 1948 and now. She can
speak in two directions when allowed.

Welcome to the history of infinite security.
She is buying cashews in the sou2 on her
way to Masjid Al-A8sa. She is being
sleeping on the cold carpeted floor.

Between yesterday and tomorrow 8uds orbits around its centre.

Sand reorienting from dome to dome.

No place more divided and invariant. No place more and.

Circling the area I become another.

Depending on
the Arabic you speak

8 is either
pronounced

or silent. The poem
dis/appears

BORDER TONGUE

BORDER TONGUE
BORDER TONGUE
BORDER TONGUE
BORDER TONGUE
BORDER TONGUE
BORDER TONGUE

After watching Mona Hatoum's
Measures of Distance

My father's love, my mother's body.
Both regenerate with astounding speed.

—LADAN OSMAN

"The scalps of the women with the best prophecies are dry this season" (2019)

Sometimes, when in a circle, if I wish to exit, I must leap.

—LAYLI LONG SOLDIER

"38" (2017)

[Buzzing of video stops. Daughter turns the hourglass.]

What do you think?

[Pause.]

[Nervous laughter.]

Did you like it?

No.

To be separated?

[Pause.]

[Buzzing of video stops. Mother turns the hourglass.]

[Pause.]

[Nervous laughter.]

Yeah 7ilo it's nice. Do I have to speak English?

It's nice ya3ni how her relationship the mother and the daughter bas t3azabu. Haram. Fi ishe mish 7ilo.

Yeah tab3an. Separated mish innu kaifhoom. They had to.

[Pause.]

Bas 2edd ma ta3edna ma3 ba3id i7na we can understand each other at the end. Especially because we are women and you are my daughter. W ba3dan kibru we understand each other not just as binit wa immha.

Was it annoying trying to focus on the Arabic?

That's why I like it.

[Long pause.]

Bi nisbi le ana I want to block the Arabic so I can understand the English. It's very hard. And you're the opposite.

Yeah 7ilo it's strange. Ma shaife hek shi 2ebbil.

[Long pause.]

[Pause.]

Before you got married did your mom talk to you?

Do you wish that she had or was it fine to hear it from other people?

[Pause.]

[Pause.]

No not my mom. Friends and sisters. Bas il imm kanet kteer 3aib ti7ki bi hadil maw9'u3. I don't think there was a single day she talked to me.

It doesn't really matter. Huwwa a7san shi bil madressi bit3alim wa7ed. To learn what's right is better than to learn alone. Especially now. It's so dangerous bit3alim eshya2 il 3'alatt min il iflam w video.

[Pause.]

Speaking of closeness and distance my thigh beside Mama's on her bed was a reminder of how far our bodies had recently been. A gap that once the conversation was over would reopen less wide. With every transcription of her voice, less wide. Less wide with every edit and reprint.

For the first and only time, my mother as a woman and her daughter as a woman. Desiring. Trying to realign.

Heaven lies beneath a mother's feet.
What is at her centre?

Is it pleasurable for the woman? Mona said.
Her mom said, Yes it is pleasurable.

I said, Is it pleasurable for the woman?
Just as it is for the man, my mom said.

Mama's pause: a sigh. From within I searched for ways to leap.

sand   too hot to stand on

sand too hot to

stand

too hot to   s + and

s – and

s and

too hot to sand   to   stand

too   s ± and   to hot

Mama finds an old camera with three hours of footage from Jordan and our first year in Canada.

I hear my child-voice. My child-voice speaking Arabic. See myself as a smooth daughter of two full parents with access to the beach a border our bodies could float on.

Mama protected me from sand all day absorbing the sun too hot to stand on. Now she was returning me. The only memory of my early life unclear whether it is first-hand or from hearing her tell it.

Repeated so many times it became a symbol I lean on.

Sand in an hourglass falls in concentric circles until the space is filled then reaches back to where it fell from. I take photos of the camera's small screen send them to Baba in Iraq.

Our WhatsApp conversation a series of heart emojis and cat videos. He narrates the poor Iraqi cats mistreated as the doves and donkeys too tired to carry the life of citizens continuously recovering holes punctured in their walls broken and fixed and broken and fixed. Cats slide against Baba's dishdasha.

He FaceTimes Mama in 2019. Pixelated faces on a screen near one another. In 1983 he wrote on the back of a photo to Mama: *I am sending you this photo of a man to be with you. I wish it were me instead.* As if it were the face of someone other than himself.

I get closer through translation.

Baba says, Prison cells in Canada are paradise compared to the ones in Syria. Mama says, I talked to him through glass. I say, Still in his boxer shorts shaving when they came to take him. Baba says, We had just immigrated. Mama says, We had just immigrated. I say, I can't unsee.

It's okay, Baba says. Draw a line and start again.

They tell us a lot in school but there's also some stuff they don't tell us. Like this new thing that I learned recently.

[Laughter.]

Oh my God that's terrible.

[Laughter.]

Where did you learn all this?

Ta3rifi xxxxxxx sar feeha hek. Six months he couldn't get near her. They gave her something to put inside herself. T3alami inti la7alik just to relax. They gave her a numbing cream and it started to make him numb too.

[Laughter.]

Ra7it shahr il 3asal wa rij3at 6ili2 shahr il za8naboot mo 3asal!

[Laughter.]

first
hand holds

second hand holds

first hand

holds first second hand

holds and holds and holds

hand holds hand holds and

holds hand

holds

first hand hand

second

I transliterate.

Mama says, Kan aswa2 yom bi 7ayati.

I don't know how to get near that or away. The darkest day of my life. Every distance migrating back.

My name, Migration, born from the conjunction of two hands: my own and the one I inherited.

[Pause.]

What is that?

Like the subconscious.

[Pause.]

[Laughter.]

[Pause.]

[Pause.]

Huwwi 7ala nefsiyya. Il 3a8l il ba6in bisht3'il.

Il 3a8l il ba6in. The inside brain.

[Pause.]

But me and my sisters ma 9ar hai il mushkili. We're Palestinian.

[Laughter.]

[Pause.]

Ma 9ar twenty minutes?

[Mother and Daughter wait for the last grains to fall.]

Mona's father could not cut through barbed wire to repossess his wife's naked body known only to him. Daughter re-enters her mother's orbit, the source of all beginnings.

Most fertile body of Palestinian women so every time a child is lost we regenerate more elastic across continents even when war begins and mailboxes explode I read her Arabic tongue in mine a line to return home.

When gallery hours are over the motor turns off. Blades can stop chasing each other in circles. In reality there is no switch.

his serrated arm
never meets
his smooth arm
never meets

never meets
her serrated arm
never meets
her smooth arm

my smooth arm
never meets
my serrated arm
never meets

Draw a line again. Unmake the line. Think of nothing but its impression.

I recorded for them this poem. I wish it were me instead.

CYCLE GENERATOR

pleasure [redacted] of our bodies [redacted] with wait to return

return pleasure of our [redacted] bodies with [redacted] to wait

wait return of our pleasure [redacted] with bodies to [redacted]

[redacted] wait of our return pleasure with [redacted] to bodies

bodies [redacted] of our wait return with pleasure to [redacted]

[redacted] bodies of our [redacted] wait with return to pleasure

pleasure [redacted] of our bodies [redacted] with wait to return

HOURGLASS PROCEDURE

Maybe it was that time she played hide-and-seek with her family friends and with only two seconds left she and that boy quickly hid under the bed together maybe xxxxxxx knew it was a bad idea maybe when xxxxxxx's brother found her he slapped her hard across the face and said maybe you shouldn't have been under the bed with that boy even if it was just a game

While waiting to come xxxxxxx wonders why

She tries again the next night

Closes her eyes and thinks of nothing but waves moving over her body

If she gets really high with a long massage beforehand

x and x and x and sex excess and yes and eyes and I's and x sand x sand x

Does any xxxxxxx know she is the same as another xxxxxxx?

One plane desiring one plane interrupting

I keep thinking about xxxxxxx's inside brain

xxxxxxx says they should study the relationship between girls raised in religious households and passivity during sex

In this irreversible way

Sand sounds louder at the beginning while it's still hitting glass

Sound of sand on glass vs. sound of sand on sand

Sand and sad and sound and send and gland and glad

OUD INTERRUPTED

OUD INTERRUPTED

OUD INTERRUPTED

OUD INTERRUPTED

OUD INTERRUPTED

OUD INTERRUPTED

OUD INTERRUPTED

While listening to Naseer Shamma's
"Sukun Al-Layl Fi Baghdad"

Waiting for the long Baghdad night to close

his arm around my body
fingers on my string

long for his night
to pull my circle inside

his body his city
circling all night long

pleasure strings of our bodies
vibrate with wait

to return us quietly
to not disrupt the centre

When night comes all I want is to write for Hajer another Hajer inside of me another hundred Hajers all concentrically folded into the same body like one circle inside another circle inside another circle inside another o inside another o

another

o

yes yes yes YES YES Y

EEEEEEE SSSSSSSSYESYESYESYESYES

YES yes yes yes yes y e s y e s y e s y e s y e s y e s y

e s y e yes yes yes yes yes yes yes !!!!!!!!!!!!!!!!!!!!!!!!!!!! yes

yes yes YES YES YES YES YES yes yes yes yes yes YES YES YES

!!!!!!!!!!!!!!!!!!!!!!!!!! yes yes yes yes yes yes yes yes yes yes YES Y

YYYYYEEEEESSSSYESYES yes yes yes yes y e s y e s y e s y e s y e s y e s

e s y e !!! yes yes yes yes yes yes yes YES YES YES

ES YES YES YES YES YES YES YES YES yes yes yes yes yes yes yes yes yes

ES YES YES YES YES YYYYYEEEEESSSS YES YES YYYYYYYYY EEEEE

SSYESYESYESYESYESYES SSSSSS YES YES YES YES YES YES YES yes yes

y e s y e s y e s y e s y e s y e s y e s y e s y e s y e s y e s y e s y e yes ye

es yes !!!!!!!!!!!!!!!!!!!!!!!!!!!!!! yes yes yes yes yes yes yes yes yes YES Y

s yes yes yes yes YES YES YES YES YES YES YES !!!!!!!!!!!!!!!!!!!!!!!!!

s yes yes yes yes yes YES YES YES YES YESYYYYYEEEEES

y e s y e s y e s y e s y e s y e s y e s y

!!!!!!! yes yes yes yes yes yes yes YES YE

YES yes yes yes yes yes y

For three minutes until

there is a hidden camera

attached to the light fixture

or between two books on the shelf

or the power goes out

or sewage overflows the streets

a bat across the ceiling

broken locks

curfew or

an American sniper

waiting to shoot me clean

For five minutes until

the mountain rocks take too many millions of years to turn into sand
manufacturers become impatient resort to lying stealing the usual things we
must make it soon before we are depleted

For twenty-seven minutes until

Baghdad Night is no longer available on Apple Music

Waiting for the long Baghdad night to replay

its grooves phantom and private
deprived we search other streaming

services our night replete with new
accounts agreements to terms

and conditions being watched we listen
lowest volume of oud strings overlap

tracks of sand around buzzing
motor shaking hand recorded at the gallery

before I knew him fully as another
stroke gone unstroked

towermountain → riverbed → sand → concrete → towermountain

Notes at the beginning return at the end

To return to Baghdad know
nothing has changed

and

To return to Baghdad
know nothing has changed

Waiting for the long Baghdad night to fall

down the mountain fold
fragments of rock for riverbed

between our homes he shields
his body over mine

storms of earth not rooted enough
eyes of sand and red sky

after it settles we sweep
a new day or the same long night

rub against other nights making
grains more and more circular

RAMADAN RECORD

RAMADAN RECORD
RAMADAN RECORD
RAMADAN RECORD
RAMADAN RECORD
RAMADAN RECORD
RAMADAN RECORD

1

My first fast doesn't count.
I masturbate twice and lie about praying.
Then I see from underneath my blinds the distant
row of houses, a streetlight, and think of Allah
closely for the first time in three years.
Of Allah as a thing I cannot be lonely for.

2
The sheikh says, Change something about yourself
to remember Allah. Wear your watch on your right hand
and think of Allah every time you see it.
I'm trying not to complain.

3
Everyone waits for a baby to be born
to hold her to smell her newborn skin
to feel her newborn toes.

I have a fried egg, labneh, za3tar, and oatmeal with dibis
for su7oor while Baba holds himself in sujood.

To feel a smallness.

4
With the bathroom fan on, my neighbour's roof,
a fleck of airplane disappearing behind it,
I drink water.

5
Too hungry to write. Too much to write to write.
Too many leftovers every night.

We wait all day to eat
and after the first three dates
and a long drink of laban
we wait to be hungry again.

6
I can't stop scrolling through food accounts on Instagram,
I say to my lover, and he says,
You know when you miss someone
you look at their photo and it helps.

He says, We don't ask other Muslims
"Are you partaking in Ramadan?"
but rather "Are you observing Ramadan?"
His hunger is so vast it clears his head
and lets him realize how angry his dad becomes
at a stray pair of shoes.

7
It's hard to celebrate without food.
I sit with my mother, my mother, my mother
and see a daughter respond to my voice.
I become motherly.
I become emptier every day.
Lost two pounds.

8

How does it feel?
Imagine you can't eat or drink for
seventeen hours.

9

10

We eat tomato soup in the name of our
dead grandfather garlic bread in the name
of our dead grandmother ma2lubi in the
name of our dead aunt.

11

I'm in transit and call my lover while he is in transit.
Our voices move through two layers of car speakerphones.
We have to say everything twice.

Baba brings me peeled tangerines at midnight.
They taste like his cologne.

12

The same stretch of King Vaughan I drove on four days ago
has now completely bloomed.

13
See some girls and fall back in love a bit with Ramadan.

14
When Baba says he is disappointed
we are not those man's children
it's all politics.

15
Through a story she tells me through a story
through six other girls I see a possible future.

I stop myself from eating more fesenjoon
even though that's all I want.

16
We eat askidinia for the first time this year
and have to say surat al-fati7a.

17
After an 3azeema in Woodbridge,
Baba says about the men,
Iraq never used to be like this.
The Iraqi men in an Iraq in Canada.

18
I dream about Mona Hatoum.
She tells me I'm not doing + *and* – justice
because there's not enough binary code.
Then she makes me mlu5iyeh
and we talk about love.

19
I observe it is possible to be + and – and and and and
when her father's arm is around her shoulder
allowing her to celebrate towards and not away.

20
The first xxxxxxx with her own home
out at night in the courtyard
we laugh uninterrupted.

21
On the first odd night, we leave Mama at the masjid
get bubble tea in Markham.
Humid and full of girls.

22

23
The sheikh says, As long as Laylit Al-8adr continues
it will contain you. Pray tonight
and it will count for one thousand prayers.

24
I cut my fast and it is over for me now.
The beginning of my cycle
marks the end of my Ramadan.

25
Red trees, oil stains, convenience store,
front lawn reconstruction, ankles.

Has your wish come true?

26
Sit and stare at a dozen graphite seas.

At the masjid a woman walks by and Mama says,
Heeyi il bit9ali feena.
She is the one who leads our prayers, but more precisely,
she is the one who prays inside us.

27
+ + + + + + + until I get home.

28

To sit on the edge of a body of water
and not be seen. Only the rhythm of gravel,
a leafless tree, crickets.

29

All day I feel my brain tightening
as if dried from the sun. I apologize to my lover.
I want his head on my lap. Sometimes I have
a word inside me and have to say it out loud:
Gobsmacking!

30

Eid

A little girl walks between the rows of praying women searching for her mother.

I still don't know if I know her.

HOURGLASS PROCEDURE

This is all I have for today

I'm sorry xxxxxxx

Why can't I do this properly anymore?

Why do I keep saying I want to be a mother?

I want to be a mother so I can tell my daughter what I never got to hear

No one taught us how to receive

Shouldn't the first thing that goes inside you be you?

I should reunite with xxxxxxx ask her why she never fingered herself

I can't get rid of this wall in my head

There's barely anything to censor

[redacted]

[redacted] I miss my mom [redacted]

Beep tests in grade nine gym

My lover's guitars

My broken clock

Leaking water into the metal popcorn bucket at Green Grotto while I wrote about Baba wearing a pink suit riding a horse in front of the pyramids

Ping-Pong in [redacted] and [redacted]'s old apartment

Things the metronome reminds me of

Why am I still stressed? [redacted]

Nothing really happened today

I don't speak Arabic because I speak English so well

I can't handle being wrong or making mistakes because everyone always expects me to be right

[redacted]

[redacted]

The beats are changing even though I know they're all the same

How am I going to be an artist when I get tired of every procedure so quickly?

GROOVES OF ONE OR MANY XXXXXXX'S

GROOVES OF ONE OR MANY XXXXXXX'S

GROOVES OF ONE OR MANY XXXXXXX'S

GROOVES OF ONE OR MANY XXXXXXX'S

GROOVES OF ONE OR MANY XXXXXXX'S

GROOVES OF ONE OR MANY XXXXXXX'S

GROOVES OF ONE OR MANY XXXXXXX'S

Girls park in a Pizza Pizza
plaza. Girl turns off the car,
sets a twenty-minute timer
on her phone. Girls shift to
find comfortable positions.

I don't use my fingers but I use my vibrator sometimes
It doesn't feel good I never used to but now I'm a
changed woman The angle of your own fingers you just
can't I've been fingering myself since I was like eleven
years old get the right angle I started masturbating
when I was really young but not properly

I'm so proud of myself

For me personally it was bad
I think it harms your sexual health

When I was five taking a bath it was the running water
my sister caught me and was like
w e d o n ' t d o t h a t

I didn't know why or what it was

Girl starts the car and turns
the heat up. Girls shift.

I don't know if I'm having an ,
You know when you're
orgasm or not
having an orgasm

What's the point then?

It feels good
It feels good

It feels good
It feels good
It feels good
It feels good

When do you stop?

When my hand gets tired

Girl turns off the car.

I've had three in the span of four minutes five in forty-five minutes ten in two hours one in three hours seven in two days sixty-three in one month two in three months zero in eight weeks

mmm same mhmm ohhh yeahh me too yess same
mmm same mhmm ohhh yeahh me too
mmm mmm mmm yeahh yes okay
yess same mmm mmm mmm yeahh yes okay

I faked my orgasm

I felt so guilty
guilty
guilty
guilty
guilty
guilty
guilty
guilty

I wanted to get it over with

Girl starts the car and turns
the heat up higher.
Shifting. Shifting.

*

Mothers and fathers downstairs.
Girls sit on the bed.

Can we takeways are you waiting?

I'm waitingshould I tell Mom?

She keeps askingwaiting for something

Just tell her we're goingis to move out

Say we're waiting for ~~xxxxxxx~~never ends

Men's voices get louder.

I want a specific align with my mom

I've expected life since I was twelve

I've imagined everything myself

I'm waiting conventional

I'm waiting most joy

in our community in our community in our community in our community you can't do that in our community

Voices downstairs and in the bedroom get quieter. Clock ticks.

+
–
+
–
+
–
+
–
+
–
+
–
+
–

I don't because I can't

It stays with you forever

Your hurt

I carry the weight of two

*

*Girls driving on the first
warm night of the year.*

I don't care if they're listening

The FBI from my computer screen

Show me an ad for a cheap teddy coat

Thank you so much

Do you remember that time?

On the street

I don't know how she knew

There's no way she saw

I think windows

I think cameras

I hide my leftover food

Like the apocalypse

Like Allah

Of the highest importance

You can come tell me but you shouldn't be telling everyone else

She's worried

I keep things private now

Everything is the end of the world

Anything that displeased her displeased me

What would I be left with

My GPS coordinates

My mother as my friend

My modesty

I missed out

I've always been

Splitting for another

Making more and more

Private

Can we open the sunroof?

Girls don't hear
the timer go off.

CYCLE GENERATOR

her Arabic tongue in [redacted] line to return home

her home Arabic in [redacted] mine to line return

her return home in [redacted] tongue to mine line

her line return in [redacted] Arabic to tongue mine

her mine line in [redacted] home to Arabic tongue

her tongue mine in [redacted] return to home Arabic

her Arabic tongue in [redacted] line to return home

her hand at twelve

her hand at six
her hand at six
her hand at six
her hand at six
her hand at six

her

hand

at

one

her hand at seven
her hand at seven
her hand at seven
her hand at seven
her hand at seven
her hand at seven
her hand at seven
her hand at seven
her hand at seven
her hand at seven
her hand at seven

REVOLUTIONS
REVOLUTIONS
REVOLUTIONS
REVOLUTIONS
REVOLUTIONS
REVOLUTIONS
REVOLUTIONS

In wanting to break the linearity, it is as if we have been forced into its opposite, to turn full circle, as if the text in this had come to its own end in itself, even were this to explode.

—NICOLE BROSSARD

The Aerial Letter (1988) (translated by Marlene Wildeman)

3AIB

xxxxxxx and xxxxxxx and

xxxxxxx

and

3aib

3aib 3aib

3aib 3aib

xxxxxxx

xxxxxxx

xxxxxxx

3aib

3aib 3aib 3aib 3aib

3aib

and and and and and and

and and and and and

and and 3aib

3aib

3aib 3aib

I have been sitting in the sand with xxxxxxx The train goes by every

twenty minutes moves grains around our feet We forget to wait We reveal

We widen the circle to make space for more xxxxxxx xxxxxxx wants to push

her finger into the sand until she touches the box xxxxxxx has to be considerate

of boundaries She says no to a date with a guy she likes She gives up

on wanting a tattoo She avoids high Arab traffic areas: anything local,

Mississauga, Blue Mountain, Niagara Falls Who will be there and

how can I sit in a way that my face won't show? xxxxxxx just wants a Costco hotdog

xxxxxxx protects her reputation xxxxxxx judges another xxxxxxx and closes herself

off for fear of being judged xxxxxxx makes a private Instagram account

only some of us can follow xxxxxxx is betrayed by the community

It is not within xxxxxxx to hide It is within xxxxxxx to hide and every day

the lies breed more lies xxxxxxx contemplates which of the lies will make

her feel less guilty One revolution of guilt:

Guilt

Guilt

Guilt

Guilt

Guilt

Guilt

Guilt

Guilt

Guilt

Guilt

Guilt

Guilt

Guilt

Guilt

Guilt

Guilt

Guilt

xxxxxxx's back hurts from sitting in the sand with no support   Which friend should
xxxxxxx say she is with today?   She said xxxxxxx two days ago
Now that we're talking about it xxxxxxx realizes she is always giving more   Am
I being a good girlfriend to you?   Is there something else you need?
xxxxxxx lets her boyfriend go a little bit longer in that position that cramps her thighs
She blames herself for not coming   It's harder for girls   Her boyfriend
can tell his mom I'm meeting xxxxxxx for lunch   xxxxxxx has done things
but her mom doesn't know she has done things   xxxxxxx prays five times a day so
she doesn't lose Allah   When allowed xxxxxxx can speak in two directions
xxxxxxx can admit she no longer eats halal   There is no border between
xxxxxxx and her parents   There are so many borders intersecting xxxxxxx
she reduces into the night   We solve for xxxxxxx but she leaps away
Her body has become light for our hands   xxxxxxx wants to be good
I want to be good too xxxxxxx   Sometimes we are

Daughterly   Daughterly

Daughterly   Daughterly

Daughterly   Daughterly

Daughterly Daughterly

Daughterly Daughterly

Daughterly Daughterly

Daughterly Daughterly

Daughterly Daughterly

Daughterly Daughterly

Daughterly Daughterly

Daughterly Daughterly

Daughterly Daughterly

Your mother is worried about what to feed her guests for brunch so you are worried

Your mother is carrying sand so you are carrying sand Your mother has had this sand

since she was a girl and saved it for you You take the sand from your mother and

forget what all other substances feel like Your mother lies to your father

for you and you let your mother lie You set an alarm to make sure you

get home on time You know your limits You know which parts to sand

Your mother is calling and you are forgetting how to call your mother

You are holding a string with your tightest possible grip until you can let go

Sand

[redacted]

Sand

[redacted]

Sand

[redacted]

Sand

[redacted]

Sand

[redacted]

Sand

[redacted]

Sand

[redacted]

Sand

[redacted]

Sand

This is not sustainable Sometimes you can't be good

The two blades around the motor are really one blade with two ends

One making grooves one unmaking the grooves One making smooth one unmaking

the smoothness and compromising how deep she wants to go I am in the sand

I am revolting in the sand at the same speed as you I am revolving

around the same centre xxxxxxx there is only one system

Of mothers and daughters Only one daughter of

mothers and systems Only one mother of daughters

and systems

Only one system of mothers and daughters

Mothers Mothers Mothers

Mothers Mothers Mothers Mothers Mothers Mothers

Mothers Mothers Mothers Mothers Mothers

You waited for your husband to leave to do your twelve-day cleanse

You missed the sun Your mother told you your father told her

your skirt is too short and you told me my father said my skirt is too short

You started when you were in the mood and finished when the sand ran out

SIFT
SIFT
SIFT
SIFT
SIFT
SIFT
SIFT

If I could say anything

I would

say it could not have been

my fault

say I created

+ and –

say I trapped you

in the sand with me

say I was scared

and all I could do was circulate

fear to you

hold you

when you were scared say

it was me

hypothetical or definitive

question or charge

say I was the cause

of all your pain

even then it could not have been

my fault my daughter

I was a mother only

in the way I knew how

to be a daughter

forced into circles

by an invisible force

I had to keep moving

my nails dragging through the dirt

became your nails

hands I passed on to you genetically

and by burden

could not have been

my fault my body

created to create

your body

I birthed you in sand

for one revolution

every revolution a new birth

every birth a new daughter

every daughter easier

to birth revolution

getting smaller and smaller

all my daughters took on

my shape I was a mother

to other mothers and fathers

daughters that weren't my own

making me more motherly

more mother

I was a mother to make more

mothers I made you

in my mother image

my fault my mirror

I washed henna out of mother's hair

with hands that lifted daughter's

feet off hot sand

with hands that peeled garlic

raw for father

kept father calm

covered his eyes before daughter

covered his ears

put him back to sleep

carried a weight only

I could see

my fault my womb

what a mess

I created sand everywhere

every line of sand for you

every line I created you destroyed

every line destroyed created

new lines pull us

together and apart

while waiting to feel

what happens at the next revolution

it could not have been

my fault my arm

could not reach

your arm

even as we connected

around the same violence

it could not have been your fault

daughter facing outward

you could not see

what holds you to the earth

we only spin in circles

until we learn

how to turn in

sift through sand

inside our bodies

observe it is the same sand

same body

NOTES

Much of *Revolutions* is a response to Mona Hatoum's artwork + *and* –, which I first encountered online in March 2016 and in person January 2019 at the exhibition *Open Works. Art in Movement, 1955-1975* at La Pedrera in Barcelona. The photo of + *and* – is reprinted with permission from Mona Hatoum's studio.

Throughout *Revolutions,* I move between English and Arabic, using the following Arabic Texting Code:

English Number	Arabic Letter
2	ء
3	ع
3'	غ
5	خ
6	ط
7	ح
8	ق
9	ص
9'	ض

The book's epigraphs are from the poem "While Waiting" in *The Butterfly's Burden* by Mahmoud Darwish, translated by Fady Joudah (Copper Canyon Press, 2007), and from the poem "Mother and Daughter" in *Something Sinister* by Hayan Charara (Carnegie Mellon University Press, 2016).

In "Hourglass Procedure," the line "If it weren't for the mirage" is excerpted from Darwish's poem "In Her Absence I Created Her Image" in *The Butterfly's Burden.*

In "Open Guide of Palestine," the epigraph is from Darwish's poem "In Jerusalem" in *The Butterfly's Burden.* The line "Soldier of Death!" is adapted from a sign that read "Danger of Death!" found on an electric tower in the Occupied

Palestinian Territories. "Welcome to the history of infinite security" is adapted from "Welcome to the future of cyber security" which appears on the website of Check Point Software Technologies, an Israeli IT security company. The line "Circling the area I become another" is adapted from the line "I walk as if I were another" in Darwish's poem "In Jerusalem."

In "Border Tongue," the first epigraph is from the poem "The scalps of the women with the best prophecies are dry this season" by Ladan Osman, originally published in Poem-a-Day by the Academy of American Poets in 2019. The second epigraph is from the poem "38" in *Whereas* by Layli Long Soldier (Graywolf Press, 2017). The line "Speaking of closeness and distance" is adapted from Mona Hatoum's statement on *Measures of Distance*, "I wanted every frame to speak of closeness and distance," in an interview with Janine Antoni (*Bomb Magazine*, 1998). The line "It's okay ... Draw a line and start again," was overheard in a teashop in England. A manager was consoling an employee who had to quit for personal reasons.

In "Oud Interrupted," many of the poems follow an oud string structure: one monostich and five couplets.

In "Revolutions," the epigraph is from *The Aerial Letter* by Nicole Brossard, translated by Marlene Wildeman (The Women's Press, 1988).

ACKNOWLEDGMENTS

First and forever, to Mustapha Safadieh: thank you for your love and support as I wrote this book and experienced its contents. Thank you for making my life brighter.

Revolutions would not be the same had I not seen + *and* – in person, so thank you to the MFA program at the University of Guelph for offering me a travel grant to visit the *Open Works* exhibition in Barcelona. Thank you to my poetry teachers, Dionne Brand and Kevin Connolly. A huge thank you to my generous mentor and thesis advisor, Margaret Christakos: your careful attention to my work and belief in me were instrumental in conceptualizing and writing the book. And to the people I learned so much from in those two years and ever since, my dear friends who read earlier versions of these poems and made the MFA program a million times better: Evelyna Ekoko-Kay, Claire Freeman-Fawcett, Rebecca Kelly, Kaitlin Reuther, Greg Rhyno, Zoe Imani Sharpe, Sheung-King, Leanne Toshiko Simpson, and Bardia Sinaee.

Oubah Osman: you deserve your own line. Thank you for offering the language I needed to frame *Revolutions*, and thank you, above all else, for your friendship.

I am indebted to the incredible team at Talonbooks who took a chance on my manuscript and spent many hours editing, designing, and caring for it. Thank you, Ryan Fitzpatrick, Rahat Kurd, Les Smith, and Catriona Strang for your patience and guidance.

It's surreal to be writing this: thank you, Mona Hatoum and your studio, not just for your permission to include a photograph of + *and* – in the book, but for taking an interest in my work and allowing me to be in conversation with yours.

Revolutions is dedicated, in part, to xxxxxxx, who holds within her all the women who shared their stories with me and all the women whose stories must remain private. Thank you, Aya, Ayaa, Ban, Deniz, Marwa, Nora, and Yasmeen. I know it's never easy and I'm so grateful for your trust. Most of all, thank you to my sisters who understand what this all means more than anyone, who cried and laughed with me in that car: Shereen, Sukiena, and Zainab. I'm so lucky to know you.

Finally, to my mom: everything came from you and everything is for you. Thank you, Mama.

HAJER MIRWALI is a Palestinian and Iraqi writer living in Toronto. She has an MFA in Creative Writing from the University of Guelph. Her work has been published in the *Ex-Puritan*, *Brick*, *Room*, and *Joyland*.